Beautiful America's
Washington

Front cover: Mount Rainier from Paradise Meadows

Published by
Beautiful America Publishing Company
P.O. Box 244
Woodburn, OR 97071

Library of Congress Catalog Number
00-023635

ISBN 0-89802-709-8
ISBN 0-89802-710-1 (paperback)

Printed in Korea

Lake Cushman, Olympic National Park

Beautiful America's
Washington
Text and Photography
by George Wuerthner

Beautiful America Publishing Company
T.M.

Contents

Introduction

For a long time most people outside of Washington dismissed the state as a scenic backwater with a lot of trees and rain, but not much else to offer in the way of culture or economic opportunity. Even "quaint" was how some characterized Seattle, the state's largest urban center. If asked what they knew about Washington, most outsiders would portray the state as the domain of loggers, salmon fishermen, and apple growers, with a few Boeing aircraft plants thrown in. Such depictions are based upon fact to some degree, and surely, Washington does have some of these features. But these ideas represent a rear view mirror perspective on the state. In the booming economic times of the 1990s, the only thing that hasn't really changed about Washington is the fact that the western part of the state still gets a lot of rain. If you have the view that Washington is a charming resource extraction outpost, think again.

Washington State has suddenly burst onto the national scene. Long-time residents have known that it's one of the most livable and beautiful states in the nation, but it seems that the rest of the nation is only now starting to recognize that fact. During the 1990s, western Washington from Olympia to Bellingham has seen unprecedented growth as people from throughout the country have flooded into the "Evergreen State" to enjoy its lifestyle and economic opportunities. Even other parts of the state such as Vancouver and Spokane have shared in this growth. Though Washington State may seem like it was tacked on to the northwest corner of the country as an afterthought, today it has a front row seat for the growing trade of the Pacific Rim, where much of the economic future of the nation is tied. Washington is a backwater no more, and has grown into one of the most vivacious and vibrant societies in America with a cultural and economic diversity that few other states can rival.

Kayaker in Olympic National Park

Mount Shuksan

The hub of the state's population and economic growth is Seattle. Posed on bluffs rising above Elliott Bay along the shore of spectacular island-studded Puget Sound, Seattle's scenic location is rivaled by only a handful of other cities in the world. Having a favorable location on the West Coast, a growing trade with Asian markets combined with its own economic engines like the software giant Microsoft, and aircraft manufacturer Boeing, Seattle sits where the future can be seen.

Yet Seattle isn't the only urban region in the state that is experiencing an economic transition. The Vancouver (Washington's) region just across the Columbia River from Portland is experiencing its own economic revival, based partly on its favorable location near Portland and at the entrance to the spectacular Columbia River Gorge.

East of the Cascades lie fertile agricultural regions that grow much of the nation's bounty of wheat and fruit. Increasingly, some of these agricultural regions like Wenatchee, Ellensburg, and Yakima are becoming retirement centers as well, as people discover the unhurried pace of the region combined with the mild dry climate as a good location to live a vigorous lifestyle during one's golden years.

Spokane anchors the state's eastern border, and is Washington's second largest city. A regional trade center, Spokane has experienced its own economic boom based upon trade, tourism and retirement connected to its inland location near the lakes and rivers of eastern Washington and northern Idaho.

Washington appears to be one of the most desirable locations in the country to live in the 21st Century, and given its favorable climate, geography and economic position, it is not difficult to understand why most Washingtonians are optimistic about their future.

Geography and Climate

S haped roughly like a rectangle with the northwest corner torn off, the state is bounded by Canada on the north, with Idaho forming its eastern border, the Pacific to the west, and Oregon and the Columbia River marking its southern border. Washington is the 20th largest state in the nation with 68,192 square miles within its bounds.

The Cascade Range is the dominant physical feature. These mountains divide the state into a dry eastern two-thirds and a wet western third. The Cascades are extremely rugged. Most of the higher peaks are volcanoes like Mount St. Helens, Mount Adams, Glacier Peak and Mount Baker. These peaks rise above 10,000 feet with Mount Rainier, the largest of the Cascade volcanoes, rising over 14,000 feet in elevation.

The northwest corner of the state contains Puget Sound, an island-studded inland sea that was once covered by a giant continental glacier. The Ice Age glaciers gouged deep channels like Hood Canal that penetrated deep into the land and left behind piles of moraine which created many of the islands that now dot the sound. Puget Sound not only moderates the climate, but also provides sheltered bays and harbors favorable to maritime shipping – a boom to western Washington's economy. Most of Puget Sound's cities lie on relatively flat glacial outwash left behind by Ice Age glaciers. Except for a few natural prairies found south of Tacoma, most of western Washington is naturally forested with giant Douglas fir, western hemlock, western red cedar, and silver fir forests.

Sticking out like a thumb into the Pacific is the Olympic Peninsula. Bound on three sides by water, the Olympics are isolated from most of the rest of Washington, despite their relatively close proximity to urban centers like Seattle. On a clear day, the Olympic Mountains provide a striking vista when viewed from

North Head Lighthouse

Opposite: The beach at Cape Disappointment

Seattle and other western Washington communities. Though less than 8,000 feet in elevation, the Olympics are extremely rugged, and rise directly from sea level. The rainy Olympic Peninsula hosts some of the largest trees found in the United States with individual record specimens of Douglas fir, western red cedar, western hemlock, and Sitka spruce among other species.

East of the Cascades, the landscape is more subdued. Known as the Columbia Plateau, it is one of the largest basalt flows in the world. Much of the region has been plowed up and transformed into orchards or wheat fields. During the last Ice Age major floods ripped across eastern Washington creating a dissected landscape today known as the Channeled Scablands.

North of the Columbia River is a forested mountainous area that extends from the arid Okanogan Valley to the Idaho border. The western portion of this region is known as the Okanogan Highlands. This region has few permanent communities and is probably the least visited region of the state.

In the northeast corner of the state, lie the rugged Selkirk Mountains, a range that extends into British Columbia. The Selkirks are renowned for their inland rainforest with large specimens of western red cedar and other typically coastal tree species that reach large dimensions in these mountains.

The Blue Mountains, a range found primarily in Oregon that barely crosses the Washington border into the southeast corner of the state, is the most Rocky Mountain like of the state's uplands, with warm summers and cold winters. The Blue Mountains are dominated by forests of grand fir, western larch, ponderosa pine and Douglas fir interspersed with grassy canyons.

Washington is a state divided. The western half lies facing on saltwater, laced with bays and rivers, and dominated by a mild, maritime climate. This climatic regime ends abruptly at the 600-mile-long north and south wall created by the Cascade Range. These mountains are a barrier to the movement of moisture-bearing clouds, and the climate east of the range is dry and sunny – with communities like Wenatchee, Walla Walla, and Yakima all boasting 300 sunny days a year. Eastern Washington, with its wheat fields and arid hills looks a lot more like parts of eastern Montana or Kansas than a place known as the "Evergreen State."

Despite its reputation as a rainy place, most of western Washington is not actually all that wet. Yes, there is moss and ferns nearly everywhere, but still the region as a whole is not nearly as wet as appearances might suggest. Seattle's annual precipitation of 38 inches is less than New York City's 44 inches or Miami's 55 inches. Although it's cloudy much of the time, places like Buffalo, New York and Burlington, Vermont experience even more gray skies, and they don't enjoy flowers blooming in March. Other parts of western Washington are even drier. Sequim on the Olympic Peninsula receives less than 20 inches of precipitation a year, making it the driest community on the entire West Coast north of Santa Barbara, California! Other communities in the San Juan Islands are similarly blessed with minimal rainfall, and mild climate.

There are, however, places in western Washington that rise to the challenge as rainy places. The western and southern sides of the Olympic Peninsula receive drenching rains, with communities like Forks recording annual precipitation often exceeding 130 inches. Wynoochee Oxbow on the southern side of the mountains once recorded 184 inches of rain in a single year! Communities adjacent to the Cascades like Issaquah are also considerably wetter than areas closer to Puget Sound, since the rising heights of the mountains wrings moisture from air masses attempting to cross the mountains. This moisture often comes as snow in the winter, and the western slope of the Cascades holds snowfall records in the United States. Mount Baker near Bellingham received more than a 1,000 inches of the white stuff during the 1998-1999 snow season setting a new North American record.

Even with all the moisture, summers are often very sunny throughout western Washington with July, August and September the driest months. This gives rise to another oddity about the region's climate. With nearly perfect sunny skies the norm in summer, and high-pressure systems parked off the coast for weeks at a time, the region's humidity remains refreshingly low.

The presence of the cool ocean waters helps to moderate the climate of western Washington. Puget Sound seldom rises above 55 degrees and the abundance of water helps to cool the air, keeping temperatures moderate throughout the region. In general, most of western Washington is characterized by a mild maritime climate with temperatures seldom dipping below freezing, even in the winter months, and snowfall is restricted to higher elevations.

Everything that is said about western Washington stops at the crest of the Cascades. Eastern Washington has a much more continental climate with occasional intrusions of cold Arctic air in winter, and frequently hot-baking summers. The Palouse Prairie region that extends from the Cascades southeast across the state to the Idaho-Oregon border has hot summers and less than 15 inches of precipitation annually. Some areas receive less than 8 inches of precipitation easily qualifying it as desert. At times it feels like a real desert. Temperatures can rise above 100 degrees and the state record of 118 degrees was recorded near Pasco in 1961. The saving grace for the region is the near absence of any humidity. Get in the shade of a cottonwood tree, and you'll feel comfortable even on a hot day. Water storage in reservoirs created by the numerous dams along the Columbia River and its major tributaries has permitted irrigated agriculture to gain a foothold despite the regional aridity.

The northern mountain tier of the state is cooler, and snowier. Daytime winter temperatures typically hover around 30 degrees with an occasional nighttime temperature that reaches zero or lower. The Okanogan Valley is typically warmer in winter, and occasionally hot in summer with temperatures sometimes exceeding 100 degrees.

As you move eastward towards the Idaho border, the average elevation increases, resulting in slightly cooler temperatures and greater moisture. This is reflected by the natural occurrence of trees that straggle westward from Spokane. Spokane itself has a pleasant year-round climate with warm, but seldom hot summers, and relatively mild winters with occasional snowfall.

Fort Canby State Park

History

Washington's mild climate and plentiful salmon supported a rich Native American culture. The tribes in Washington represented many different linguistic groups – the result of numerous invasions of the area by a variety of tribal affiliations. Nevertheless, no matter where they came from, nearly all tribes adopted similar lifestyle patterns based upon the available natural resources.

Coastal tribes enjoyed plentiful food supplies including fish, shellfish, and marine mammals. They lived communally in wooden longhouses that typically sheltered several families. The abundant foods allowed people to remain in relatively permanent villages and provided the leisure time to develop a rich cultural tradition. The bounty of food also permitted development of a slave trade, with warfare being one of the major means of slave acquisition. Inland, beyond the Cascades, salmon though still abundant, did not support permanent year-round habitation. Native people tended to be slightly more nomadic following seasonal food resources across the region.

European exploration of the region began in 1592 when Juan de Fuca, a Greek sailing under the Spanish flag, led an expedition along the coast of Washington and "discovered" the Inland Passage now named for him. Remarkably, several hundred years passed before any further European sailors plied the shores of Washington. In 1775, another Spanish expedition under Bruno de Heceta and Juan Francisco de la Bodega y Quadra landed on Destruction Island near present-day Olympic National Park, claiming the entire Northwest in the name of Spain, while losing seven men to Indian attack.

At the same time that the Spanish were attempting to lay claim to the Pacific Northwest, the English were also roaming the coast. In 1776, Captain Cook charted the entire Pacific Northwest from Oregon to Alaska (Cook Inlet near

Puget Sound sunset

Anchorage is named for him). Later in 1787 and 1788, members of the original Cook Pacific Northwest Expedition were back to investigate the region. Charles Barkley explored and named the Strait of Juan de Fuca, while John Meares named Mount Olympus. The American claim to the region came with the discovery of the Columbia River by Robert Gray in 1792. Gray named the river for his ship the *Columbia*.

In the same year that Gray was plying the waters of the Pacific Northwest, another English expedition under the command of Captain George Vancouver was probing the waters of Puget Sound and northward into Canada. Vancouver, besides contributing his name to a Washington city, a Canadian city, and an island, also named many of the features in the region including Mount Rainier, Puget Sound, Whidbey Island and Mount Baker among others.

Though the coastal waters of the region were reasonably well-known by 1800, no one had traveled overland to the region. In 1804, the Lewis and Clark Expedition set out from St. Louis, Missouri, traveling up the Missouri River and down the Columbia to the ocean. They first tried to set up a winter camp near Cape Disappointment on the Washington coast, but later moved across the Columbia to the Oregon side where they remained the rest of the winter of 1805-1806. In the spring they retraced their route arriving back in St. Louis in 1806.

The Lewis and Clark Expedition not only opened up the West, but also alerted fur trappers about the wealth in animal skins that could be obtained in the region. By the 1820s, the Hudson Bay Company had constructed Fort Vancouver, a major trading post on the Columbia River near present-day Vancouver. Other trading posts were constructed at Fort Spokane, Fort Nisqually, and Fort Okanogan. These posts helped to solidify the British claim to the Oregon Territory that included Washington State.

The British claim to the region was weakened by the overland migration of thousands of settlers on the Oregon Trail. Between 1840 and 1860 more than 53,000 people moved to Oregon Territory, most to start a new life in the

Willamette Valley. Increasing tensions between British and Americans over control of the Oregon Territory eventually led to an 1846 treaty that recognized the 49th parallel as the boundary between American and British lands. The 49th parallel remains as the boundary between Canada and the United States. The resolution of territorial claims prompted American settlement north of the Columbia River. In 1849, only 304 Americans lived north of the Columbia, but by 1853 there were nearly 4,000 U.S. citizens within what is today Washington. Washington Territory was split off of Oregon Territory in 1853. At this time, Washington Territory also included Idaho and most of western Montana as well. By 1864, these other regions were stripped off of Washington Territory creating the present state boundaries.

In 1889, Washington Territory was admitted to the Union as the 42nd state. By 1910, the population had grown to over a million people. Most of the growth was spurred by several events. The construction of the Northern Pacific and Great Northern railways during the 1880s spurred economic and population growth. The discovery of gold in the Yukon in 1898 and other strikes just after the turn of the century in Alaska, gave Washington a pivotal role as a supply source for miners and others who went north lured by gold. War played a major role in Washington's growing diversified economy. Shipping, airplane construction, and manufacturing based upon inexpensive hydroelectric power all contributed to new booms in the state.

By the 1990s, Washington's economy was quickly leaving behind its natural resource extraction roots. High tech industry, Pacific Rim and regional trade, finance, real estate, and a growing service industry all provided new employment opportunities. The state's population is now nearly 6 million. With the growing population comes the challenges of congestion, pollution, unregulated growth, strip malls, and rampant development. Whether Washington can successfully cope with these stresses, while maintaining the high quality of life for which the region is renowned, remains to be seen.

Wildlands and Parks

Despite its rainy weather, Washingtonians love to recreate outdoors. The Mountaineers, a hiking and climbing club based in Seattle, was established in 1906 setting the trend towards outdoor and mountain exploration that remains a strong tradition even today.

One of the major factors contributing to the state's livability and outdoor reputation is its public lands. The U.S. Forest Service administers the largest segment of public land, some 9 million acres. The national forests of Washington contain 24 wilderness areas that are managed to retain their primitive and undeveloped character.

The largest of these include the Glacier Peak Wilderness. Over a half million acres in size, the Glacier Peak Wilderness straddles the northern Cascades and includes its namesake mountain Glacier Peak, one of the most prominent and remote of the Cascades volcanoes. There are more than 200 lakes in the wilderness, many still unnamed, and more active glaciers than any other part of the contiguous United States. Steep glacially carved and densely forested valleys give way to alpine tundra and snowfields at higher elevations. In many places, 2,000-foot cliffs drop sharply into the valleys below. The most popular trails follow the major river corridors including the Suiattle, Sauk, White Chunk, White and Stehekin rivers. The Pacific Crest Trail wanders north-south through the length of this wilderness.

The 530,000-acre Pasayten Wilderness is the second largest Forest Service wilderness in Washington. It is 10 to 23 miles north to south and 54 miles at its widest east-west distance. Lying east of the Cascade Crest, it's considerably drier and less glaciated than the Glacier Peak Wilderness. In vegetation, terrain, and "feel" it is much more reminiscent of the Northern Rockies of Idaho or Montana

Opposite: Sea stacks at Ruby Beach

than what people conjure up when they think of Washington. Though there are few glaciers remaining among these mountain peaks, the evidence of glaciation is etched deeply upon the land. More than 160 glacially carved lakes dot the high country, and deep U-shaped glacial valleys like the wilderness's namesake, the Pasayten River, occupy former glacial troughs. There are more than 600 miles of trails in the Pasayten Wilderness, but the longest is the 73-mile Boundary Trail that straddles the U.S. and Canada border, hence its name. A segment of the Pacific Crest Trail winds through the wilderness, reaching its northern terminus just over the border in Canada.

The 400,000-acre Alpine Lakes Wilderness is the fourth largest wilderness area in Washington. Alpine Lakes Wilderness area lies between I-90 on the south and Highway 2 on the north. Directly west of Seattle with some trailheads less than an hour from downtown, it's not surprising that this is one of the most popular wildlands in the state. The other reason for its high use is a consequence of its stunning beauty. With more than 700 lakes, glaciated basins, and sharp, angular peaks, throughout the early part of the century the area was frequently mentioned as a potential new national park. In 1976, wilderness designation provided protection from development that supporters sought, and the park movement for the area died. There are numerous access points to the wilderness, with trailheads at Snoqualmie Pass along I-90 providing the easiest and quickest point of entry. Other major entry points include the Icicle River outside Leavenworth, the South Fork of the Skykomish near Stevens Pass, and Middle Fork of the Snoqualmie River. The Pacific Crest Trail also traverses the entire wilderness south to north.

The Forest Service also administers lands at Mount St. Helen's National Monument and in the Columbia Gorge Scenic Area.

Washington is home to some of the best known national parks in the country including Olympic National Park, Mount Rainier National Park and North Cascades National Park along with a number of national historic parks like Klondike Gold Rush, Whitman Mission, and Fort Vancouver. These internationally known parks draw visitors from around the globe and are the foundation for Washington's vibrant tourist industry.

Olympic National Park encompasses some 900,000 acres with nearly all of it designated wilderness. With the exception of a few roads that penetrate into the interior like the Hurricane Ridge Road, and the roads up drainages like the Hoh, Queets, and Elwah drainages, most of the park's backcountry is undeveloped. This includes some 60 miles of "wilderness" beaches, the longest stretch of undeveloped beachfront in the western United States outside of Alaska. These wild beaches are among the park's most popular hiking destinations. Although a few short trails cut across headlands, most of the hiking occurs on the beach. Other popular trails in the park include the 20-mile path up the Hoh Valley to Mount Olympus, accessing the most spectacular old-growth rainforest in the park, and the route up the Quinault River to the waterfall-studded, emerald green Enchanted Valley.

Mount Rainier is Washington's high point, and the centerpiece for Mount Rainier National Park. Though only 235,612 acres, the park contains 27 named glaciers, more than 380 lakes, and hundreds of rivers and streams. The park also has 300 miles of maintained trails. The highlight of the trail system is the Wonderland Trail that completely encircles the mountain, passing through forested valleys and across the flank of many mountain meadows. Probably no other trail route offers so much continuous alpine scenery as this one. Those attempting to complete the circuit typically allow themselves at least a week, though 10 days provides for a more enjoyable and leisurely trip.

The last major national park is North Cascades National Park complex that includes the park and two national recreation areas – Lake Chelan and Ross Lake. Taking in nearly 700,000 acres, the complex sits on the Cascade Crest just south of the Canadian border. This is some of the wildest, most inaccessible terrain in the entire state, and few trails actually penetrate the park. Access to much of the park's backcountry requires use of mountaineering skill and equipment.

Mount Rainier from Tipsoo Lake

The deep, glacial carved Stehekin River Valley is one of the most isolated in the park, requiring a boat ride down the 50-mile-long Lake Chelan to access the trailhead. Boats are also often used to access the Big Beaver and Little Beaver Trailheads off of Ross Lake. If a pick-up is arranged ahead of time, a beautiful loop up one trail and down the other can be experienced. If you do this loop, be sure to take the time to climb the 56 switchbacks to the 5,206-foot Whatcom Pass where you will be rewarded with breathtaking views of the Challenger Glacier and the rugged and aptly named Picket Range.

Other federal lands that are important for the state's quality of life include national wildlife refuges, national recreation areas, and national oceanic preserves.

Region by Region
Puget Sound

The Puget Sound region encompasses the western slope of the Cascades, the San Juan Islands, and is flanked on the east by the Olympic Peninsula. Within this region lie most of the state's largest cities including Seattle, Tacoma, Bellevue, Everett, Federal Way, Olympia and Bellingham.

With more than a half million people within the city limits, Seattle is the cultural and economic hub of the state. The city is spectacularly located on a strip of land sandwiched between the blue waters of Puget Sound and 18-mile-long Lake Washington. Look in any direction on a clear day and you will see snow-capped mountains. Within a few hours drive are national parks like Mount Rainier and Olympic. It doesn't take visitors long to figure out that Seattle is prime real estate.

Named for Chief Sealth or Seattle, the young town was established in 1851 on Elliott Bay. Lumber was the first source of trade, with most of it going south to help build another west coast city then booming under a gold rush – San Francisco. Logs were skidded down Yesler Street in the old part of Seattle to sawmills on the bay. Yesler Street became known as "skid row" when this old section of town was later inhabited by the down and out, and alcoholics.

The new town grew slowly at first, and did not distinguish itself from any of the other communities on Puget Sound, vying for growth and commerce. Indeed, Seattle suffered an economic blow when the Northern Pacific Railroad chose Tacoma as the western terminus for their line, leaving Seattle pondering about its economic future. Seattle rejoiced a few years later when the Great Northern Railroad pulled into town in 1893, linking the city with markets in the East and stimulating its role as a major port.

Seattle continued to grow as a regional distribution center, serving as an outlet for timber, fishery, farm, and mining products shipped to other parts of the world. It was World War II that really sent the city on a new trajectory. At the outbreak of the war, less than 4,000 people worked in the Boeing Airplane plants, but by 1944 more than 50,000 people were employed. Its fortunes rose and fell with various military conflicts, but eventually, Boeing changed from manufacturing largely military aircraft to its popular civilian craft like the 727 and 747 jets, giving rise to a more stable demand and employment.

In 1962, Seattle hosted the World's Fair, which drew over 9.5 million people to the city. The site now known as the Seattle Center features the Opera House, Playhouse, Pacific Science Center, as well as such well-known tourist attractions as the Space Needle, Monorail, and Coliseum.

Another Seattle icon is the Pike Street Market. Organized in 1907, the market today hosts more than 250 businesses. Originally a farm produce and fish market, today one is likely to find T-shirts and post cards for sale as well as food to eat. Strolling musicians, streetside acts, vaudevillians and magicians add to the color and atmosphere. The market is a lively and wonderful place to stroll for visitors and residents alike.

Pioneer Square is another downtown attraction. It is the oldest section of the city, and today features a small park with totem poles, and the Klondike Gold Rush Visitor Center.

For a fantastic view, and to see some of the city's older Victorian homes, a visit to Queen Anne Hill can reward one on a clear day with views of the city framed by the backdrop of Mount Rainier.

One of the biggest tourist attractions in the city is the Chittenden Locks that connect Puget Sound with Lake Washington. People come to watch the movement of ships back and forth in the lock and the migration of salmon that still swim from the ocean to spawn in tributaries of Lake Washington.

Part of this waterway is Lake Union that connects Lake Washington to the ocean.

Puget Sound Ferry, San Juan Islands

Opposite: Strait of Juan de Fuca

Lake Union is the site of a particularly "Seattle" lifestyle – the houseboat. Docks built into the lake provide the moorage for hundreds of houseboats. Once inexpensive housing for a generation of bohemian artists and musicians, today, the residents of these floating homes are more likely to be upscale residents with high-paying jobs.

Stretching along the shores of Lake Washington is the campus of the University of Washington, the state's largest and best-known university. Begun in 1861, the campus was the setting for the 1909 Alaska-Yukon-Pacific Exposition. In exchange for the use of the campus, the exposition's developers constructed a number of new buildings on the campus and helped to landscape the grounds.

The growing academic excellence of western Washington's colleges and universities is one building block of the state's new economic growth, since high tech industries are attracted to university campuses to hire highly trained and educated workers and to utilize their research facilities.

Although it's not nearly as rainy in Seattle as is reputed, the skies are often cloudy and perhaps this is one reason why the city is known for its coffee houses and bookstores; people spent a lot of time inside contemplating the weather and socializing. But when the sun does shine, the region's lakes are dotted with sailboats, bike paths are clogged with runners and mountain bikes, and trailheads at all the nearby hiking areas are full.

The surrounding suburbs like Bellevue, Bothell, Edmonds, Kirkland, Federal Way, Renton, and Redmond collectively have a larger population than Seattle. Most function as bedroom communities, although increasingly they are developing their own industrial and business bases.

Seattle's long time rival is Tacoma and for years it sat in the shadow of its larger neighbor to the north as the blue collar industrial district of the state. But Tacoma is experiencing a regrowth in civic pride and a diversified economy that is giving the community much to brag about. Home to a revitalized downtown, numerous historic homes and a 700-acre park, and little more than an hour's drive to Mount

Rainier National Park, Tacoma is increasingly seen as a desirable place to live.

Swedish settler Nicholas Delin, who operated a sawmill on the site of the future city, founded Tacoma in 1852. General Morton McCarver purchased a tract of land near the growing town, and named the site Commerce City. But the older name Tacoma – after an Indian word for Mount Rainier – remained in common usage and gradually became the accepted name. With the coming of the Northern Pacific Railway in 1873, the town's future was sealed. It quickly grew as a lumber and shipping port. Today Tacoma is one of the largest shipping container ports in the world.

Beyond Tacoma and Seattle, Olympia is a small town for a state's capital, with less than 40,000 residents. But government runs the show here, with more than 44 percent of Thurston County employed in the public sector. Olympia, like other Puget Sound communities, was founded early. The first settlers arrived here in 1846. In 1853, Washington Territory Governor Isaac Stevens named Olympia the territorial capital. Over the years, other communities tried to wrest control of the government away from Olympia, and it wasn't until 1890 that Olympia was officially designated as the state's capital.

North of Seattle lies Everett. Like Tacoma, Everett is more an industrial town than cultural center. Everett became a Weyerhaeuser timber town in 1903, with pulp and saw mills dominating the economy. Labor unrest lead to the "Everett Massacre" in 1916 when seven workers died during protests. Today the city is known for Boeing plants and as a bedroom community for commuters working in Seattle.

Heading north along the I-5 corridor is Mount Vernon, named for George Washington's Virginia estate. The community borders the Skagit River, the second largest river in the state in terms of water volume; only the Columbia is larger. The Skagit is well known for its runs of salmon and steelhead, plus bald eagles, and whitewater rafting. In winter, there are thousands of snow geese that gather on the lower river along with hundreds of eagles.

The rich farmland along the Skagit River is also renowned for its spring blossom of tulips and daffodils. The annual 10-day Tulip Festival each April attracts thousands of visitors to admire the multi-colored flowers.

Some travelers take the leisurely route along Chuckanut Drive when going north from Mount Vernon to Bellingham. Part of the old coastal highway system, the road today hugs the side of Chuckanut Mountain and offers outstanding views of the San Juan Islands on a clear day. It provides a leisurely entrance into Bellingham, home to Western Washington State University. Victorian homes, and cottages dominate the older sections of Bellingham. Sitting on Bellingham Bay with Mount Baker as a backdrop, many consider Bellingham the most attractive community in the state. For those who love mountain landscapes, within easy reach of the town are Mount Baker and the North Cascades National Park.

To the west of Bellingham are the San Juan Islands. Situated at the intersection of the Strait of Georgia, Strait of Juan de Fuca, and Puget Sound, the 172 named islands are well-known for their slower pace and quiet setting. The San Juans, originally settled by small subsistence farmers and fishermen, are increasingly attractive for retirees, bicyclists, and walkers who find the rural settings and ocean views enchanting. This is bed and breakfast country. Most of the San Juan Islands are only accessible by ferry and private boat, but a few are on the main highway system. Whidbey Island is one of these. Coupeville on the island is a designated National Historic District. Long the home of sea captains and sailors, residents and tourists alike celebrate the beautiful Victorian homes of the community.

Of the islands accessible by Washington State Ferry, Lopez is known as a biker's paradise. Its gentle terrain and lack of traffic makes it ideal for cycling. Orca Island, named for the resident killer whales of the islands, contains the highest mountain in the San Juan group, 2,409-foot Mount Constitution. The mountain is located in 4,605-acre Moran State Park, the largest park in the San Juan Island group.

Opposite: Lime Kiln Lighthouse, San Juan Island

Fawn in Olympic National Park

Daffodil farm near Mount Vernon

Opposite: Pacific Crest Trail, Alpine Lakes Wilderness

Mount Rainier, Mount Rainier National Park

Opposite: Mount Shuksan

The largest island in the group is San Juan Island. With its size of some 20 miles long and 7 miles wide, the island is home to over 5,000 residents. Most of them live in Friday Harbor, accessible by ferry from the mainland. On the west side of the island lies Lime Kiln Point State Park; the only park in the country set aside primarily to facilitate whale watching. The picturesque lighthouse at the park is also an attraction.

San Juan Island is the site of the "Pig War" commemorated by San Juan National Historic Park. At the time the war started, San Juan Island was claimed as both American and British Territory. Just who should have jurisdiction came to a head in 1859 when an American, Lyman Cutler, killed a pig owned by the Hudson Bay Company. Cutler claimed the pig was continuously rooting up his garden. The British demanded that Cutler pay for the pig, which he refused. They then demanded he come to Victoria to stand trial. Cutler rebuffed the British authorities claiming that San Juan Island was under American rule. He requested protection from the American government, and a company of soldiers was quickly dispatched to the island. The British responded in kind, and soon had several thousand troops and five warships stationed at the island. Fortunately cooler heads prevailed, and both sides agreed to settle the dispute by negotiations. Eventually it was decided that San Juan Island would remain under American rule.

Olympic Peninsula

Many Washington residents would agree that the Olympic Peninsula is one of the most beautiful parts of the state. With wild rocky beaches, and high glaciated mountains, the 6,500-square-mile peninsula is a world apart. Highway 101 provides a circular route that accesses numerous communities and parks that are located on the peninsula. The central feature of the peninsula is the Olympic Mountains. The highest point, Mount Olympus is just shy of 8,000 feet elevation,

Opposite: Tatoosh Range

yet is covered by huge glaciers. The glaciers as well as the world famous Olympic rainforest are fed by heavy precipitation coming off the Pacific Ocean. Some parts of the mountains are thought to get in excess of 200 inches of precipitation a year. Most of the Olympic Mountains are protected within Olympic National Park. The park also protects some of the finest examples of old growth Douglas fir, Sitka spruce, and western hemlock forests in the world. The Hoh rainforest is a drippy, moss-covered, emerald cathedral of ancient trees that is home to the some of the largest individual specimens of trees found in the world. The park is a United Nation's designated "Man and the Biosphere Reserve" site, recognizing the biological importance of its ancient forests.

Outside of the park, much of the timberland is within the Olympic National Forest managed by the U.S. Forest Service, Washington State, Indian Reservations, or is owned by private timber companies. Unfortunately, outside the park, loggers have scalped nearly all forested lands, and few of the magnificent ancient trees seen in the park are found outside of its protective boundaries.

Interestingly, though most of the peninsula experiences tremendous amounts of precipitation, the driest place in the entire west coast north of southern California is found here as well. Sequim on the northeast corner of the peninsula receives less than 20 inches of rainfall annually. The mild climate and abundant sunshine have transformed this former agricultural community into a major retirement area.

The Spaniard, Juan Francisco de Eliza, named Port Angeles, the largest community on the peninsula. Hudson Bay Company trappers originally settled Port Angeles and the town eventually grew into a lumber and shipping center. Today it has a diverse economy based upon timber, tourism, county, state and federal government, shipping, and retirement living. The drive from Port Angeles to Hurricane Ridge in Olympic National Park offers outstanding vistas into the heart of the Olympic Mountains.

If you want to get a feel for how it can rain on the peninsula, try the former logging town of Forks. The western-most incorporated city in the lower 48 states, Forks has one main street and about 3,800 residents. Logging used to thrive here, but in recent years the community has diversified its economy based in part upon its relative proximity to the western valleys of Olympic National Park and the coastal beaches.

A community just barely on the peninsula is historic Port Townsend. Known for its Victorian architecture, the community has some 70 buildings on the national historic register. Popular with visitors, there are more than a dozen bed and breakfasts in the town. At the entrance to Puget Sound, Port Townsend's beginnings are based upon its location as a port and guardian for the rest of the sound. Military bases, now state parks, are located on several sides of the community.

Beyond The Olympics

South of the Olympic Peninsula, the coastline of Washington has few harbors and is dominated by flat sandy beaches. One exception is Grays Harbor. The communities of Aberdeen and Hoquiam are located here. Robert Gray, who also located and named the Columbia River, discovered the harbor. The harbor, combined with the abundant forests nearby, provided the foundation for the local economy.

The only other major indentation on the Washington coast south of Grays Harbor is Willapa Bay, one of the least-developed estuaries on the west coast. The bay is well-known for its oysters, and wildlife. Part of the bay is protected from future development in the 12,000-acre Willapa Bay National Wildlife Refuge.

The Long Beach Peninsula encloses the bay. The 28-mile narrow strip of land is claimed to be one of the "longest beaches in the world." Long a popular summer destination, the miles of sandy beaches attract ocean lovers from both Washington and nearby Oregon.

Klickitat River, Wild and Scenic Area

Icicle River Valley near Leavenworth

The Bavarian shops of Leavenworth

Sullivan Lake in the Selkirk Mountains

At the southwestern tip of the state near the mouth of the Columbia the land rises to headlands now part of Fort Canby State Park. Lewis and Clark first saw the Pacific Ocean near here before moving to the Oregon side to spend the winter. The old fort used to protect the mouth of the Columbia from foreign invaders, but today the popular park is a favorite for those who come to comb the beaches, watch for whales or visit the two lighthouses found here.

The Columbia River and Gorge

From Fort Canby State Park one can travel up the Columbia River following the path of the Lewis and Clark Expedition to Vancouver, former site of the Hudson Bay Company headquarters. Vancouver today is a thriving sister city to Portland just across the Columbia River. Right on the I-5 corridor, and a two-time winner of "All American City" status, Vancouver is the economic anchor of this portion of the state.

Vancouver is also gateway to the Columbia Gorge, one of the most spectacular river canyons in America. The 60-mile-long gorge is now a national scenic area, with restrictions on development designed to maintain the scenic qualities of the region. The Columbia River is the only low elevation passage across the Cascades, and has been used as a transportation corridor for thousands of years. Highways, railroad tracks and barge traffic all contribute to the river's reputation as a major transportation link between the coast and interior of the Pacific Northwest.

Despite all this traffic, the gorge has maintained its scenic qualities and is well-known for its recreational opportunities. Be it just a scenic drive or more active participation, the gorge has something to offer almost everyone. As a hiking destination, the gorge's numerous trails are hard to beat, with paths leading to hidden glens, dramatic waterfalls, and fantastic vistas. The nearly constant winds that are funneled up through the gorge have also made the area the wind surfing capitol of the Pacific Northwest.

Opposite: Mount St. Helens

Japanese Garden at University of Washington Arboretum

Officers Row, Fort Vancouver

Climber on Mount Baker glaciers

Mount Baker

Wetlands along the Nisqually River

Opposite: Old growth forest along Tahoma Creek

Cascade Range near Washington Pass

Opposite: Lake Crescent, Olympic National Park

Victorian home in Hoquiam

Opposite: Snoqualmie Falls and Salish House Lodge

Road to Hurricane Ridge, Olympic National Park

Mountain goat in Olympic National Park

Royal Basin, Olympic National Park

Skamania Lodge, Columbia River Gorge

Opposite: Dawn on the Kettle River Range

Autumn at Dog Falls, Gifford Pinchot National Forest

Opposite: Naches River, Wenatchee National Forest

Bridge of the Gods, Columbia River Gorge

Opposite: Columbia River near Marcus

Even if you are not a participant, many people just love to sit and watch the colorful sails darting back and forth across the river propelled by the high winds that sweep through the gorge. Wildflower enthusiasts find the gorge one of the best places in the state to stroll among myriads of blossoms.

Cascades

The Cascades are among the most spectacular mountains in the West, if not the world, and much of the higher elevations of the range is protected as a national park, national monument, or national forest wilderness areas. The North Cascades National Park is known for its rugged, glaciated mountains and alpine meadows. Indeed, Washington's Cascades are so steep and snowy, they have created an immense barrier to east-west travel. Though the mountains of Colorado are much higher, there are far more year-round passes across the Rockies than exist in the Washington Cascades. In winter, there are only two major passes open to highway traffic; Stevens Pass and the I-90 corridor through Snoqualmie Pass. However, the most scenic route is the North Cascades Highway – open only in summer – offering numerous spectacular vistas of the park. Another road that dead-ends in the mountains is the Mount Baker Highway east of Bellingham. It takes you to one of the most photographed mountains in the state, 9,127-foot Mount Shuksan.

South of North Cascades National Park lies a number of magnificent wilderness areas, including Glacier Peak and the Alpine Lakes Wilderness. Motors are prohibited in wilderness areas, so access is by hiking or horseback. Fjord-like, and more than 50 miles long, Lake Chelan offers yet another way to explore the Cascades. The lake is 1,486 feet deep, making it the third deepest body of water in the United States. Scenic boat rides to the village of Stehekin are particularly popular with visitors. Many visitors opt for lunch in the village and the return boat ride to Chelan, while others put on a pack and hike into North

Cascades National Park or the nearby Glacier Peak Wilderness.

One of the best bases for exploration of these wildlands is Leavenworth, Washington. Leavenworth has fashioned its downtown on a Bavarian Village motif complete with hand carved wooden architecture, and flowerpots along the streets. The Bavarian theme even applies to clothing with men in lederhosen not an uncommon sight at stores and restaurants. The town provides outdoor recreation both in summer and winter. River running, hiking and mountain biking are popular in summer, while downhill skiing at Stevens Pass and Mission Ridge ski areas draw people in winter.

South of Snoqualmie Pass and I-90, lies Mount Rainier National Park. The park encompasses 14,411-foot Mount Rainier, highest peak in the entire Cascade Range and in Washington State. More than 2 million people visit the mountain annually, and for good reason. The mountain contains the largest concentration of glaciers outside of Alaska, plus some of the richest wildflower meadows found in the entire Pacific Northwest. To stroll among the luxuriant flower gardens at Paradise or Sunrise are unforgettable experiences. There are over 300 miles of hiking trail in the park, with the 95-mile around the mountain Wonderland Trail popular with those wanting to sample the park's backcountry.

Rainier is the largest of the Cascade volcanoes, but Mount St. Helens is the best known. When the volcano blew up in 1980, it provided Washington residents and the rest of the world, through television, a firsthand opportunity to experience the effects of a major eruption. More than 60,000 acres of forest was flattened instantly. Ash was blown across the state and its neighboring states, piling up to more than 8 inches in some places – snowplows were called out to clear the highways. The heat of the eruption melted glaciers on the mountain's flank sending huge floods cascading down the area's rivers. Designated Mount St. Helens National Volcanic Monument in 1982, the area was opened for visitation by the public and is a popular tourist spot today.

Near St. Helens lies 12,276-foot Mount Adams, a smaller version of Rainier.

Spokane River, Riverside State Park

Oregon Trail Wagon, Whitman National Historic Site

It experiences far fewer visitors since all access is via dirt logging roads, plus part of the mountain is on the Yakima Indian Reservation. The Mount Adams Wilderness is laced with hiking trails throughout its 42,280 acres. For those of a more adventurous nature, the climb up Mount Adams is one of the easiest high peaks to ascend in the Pacific Northwest. Though it is considered a "walk up," the climb to the summit does involve crossing some steep snowfields and a 6,000-foot elevation gain.

East of the Cascades

Whether you travel east through the gorge or across one of the Cascade passes, once you are east of the mountains, things dry out. The lush, dense forests of the west side give way to more open stands of ponderosa pine or grasslands. The often-cloudy skies west of the mountains change to blue on the eastern slope. There are many that believe the eastern part of Washington is the only place to live – you leave the moss and mold behind. Among the largest communities are Yakima, Ellensburg, and Wenatchee. But none of these towns are huge, with Yakima's 58,000 people being the largest community on the east slope of the Cascades. This is a region with some breathing room.

The foundation of the regional economy is its arid climate; with the two pillars being fruit orchards and retirement living. Wenatchee, for instance, gets more than 300 sunny days a year – giving it a climate more in common with someplace like Arizona than "rainy" Washington. And Yakima has a 200-day growing season. It's no wonder that the region is famous for its apples, pears, cherries, peaches, apricots, and other fruit orchards. The major fruit growing regions include the Okanogan Valley, the Columbia Valley near Wenatchee and Yakima. Wenatchee claims to be the apple capital of the world, and in the spring when the apple blossoms cover the hills and valley it is easy to believe. Not surprisingly, Washington produces 60 percent of the nation's apples.

Once you get away from the mountains, you enter the Columbia Plateau. The Columbia River and its tributaries drain most of the plateau. For most of its length, the Columbia is dammed and pooled in reservoirs. One stretch, the Hanford Reach, remains free flowing and is being proposed for Wild and Scenic River status.

The largest cities along the Columbia in this region are the tri-cities of Pasco, Richland and Kennewick. Located at the confluence of the Columbia, Yakima and Snake Rivers, their combined population makes this the fourth largest metropolitan area in the state. Richland, dubbed "Atomic City," began as a secret settlement for scientists and others working on nuclear research at the Hanford Atomic Works Site. At its height more than 60,000 workers were relocated to the region to construct and work in the facility. For decades money poured into the local economy to fund plutonium production, nuclear waste management and other research at the Hanford Site. The facility was closed in 1988, but a legacy of radioactive waste and improper disposal that was covered up for decades now makes the Hanford Site one of the biggest hazardous waste cleanup sites in the nation – ironically bringing even more federal dollars pouring into the region.

Upstream from the Hanford Reach lies Grand Coulee Dam, more than a mile long, and one of the largest construction projects ever undertaken in the United States. One of more than 200 dams that now sit on the Columbia River and its tributaries, Grand Coulee was constructed during the Great Depression as a make work project that employed thousands of people. Today the dam provides hydroelectric power, and subsidized irrigation water for thousands of acres of farmlands – to grow crops that farmers in other parts of the country are often paid not to grow.

The reservoir created by the dam, Lake Roosevelt, is now part of the Grand Coulee National Recreation Area (NRA). The NRA sprawls east and north more than 150 miles reaching almost to the Canadian border. The NRA and lake is a

Haystack Butte, Columbia River Gorge

Opposite: Pend Oreille River

popular area for boating, camping, sailing, and fishing.

All across the middle of the state are numerous dry river channels known as the Channeled Scablands that resulted from terrific deluges during the last Ice Age. Grand Coulee is just one of these ancient river channels. The Channeled Scablands were created when a glacial dam gave way on the Clark Fork River near the present Idaho-Montana border, releasing immense catastrophic flood waters to race across the lowlands of eastern Washington. More than 40 times, the ice dam gave way, each time sending a huge wall of water crashing across eastern Washington to the Columbia River. The Columbia River Gorge was scoured up to a 1,000 feet above the current river level, and chunks of ice carried by the floods were left high and dry in the Willamette Valley nearly as far south as Eugene, Oregon.

North of the Columbia River and Grand Coulee NRA lies a nearly uninhabited mountainous-forested area that includes the Okanogan Highlands, Kettle Range, and Selkirk Mountains. Much of this area lies within the Colville Indian Reservation, and Colville National Forest. The few small towns that are scattered through the area like Curlew, Colville, Republic, and Kettle Falls were once mining and logging based communities. The entire area is an outdoor paradise with numerous opportunities for hunting, fishing, hiking, camping, and boating. With the Cascades getting the bulk of the state's recreational attention, this region seems more remote and less crowded. One of the attractions is the seldom visited Salmo-Priest Wilderness on the border of Idaho and Washington, home to grizzly, woodland caribou and other species rare or non-existent in the rest of the state.

Eastern Washington

The major population center in eastern Washington is Spokane. Straddling the Spokane River, the town had its start in 1810 as "Spokane House," a trading post built by David Thompson. Today the bustling city of more than 350,000 (counting suburbs) is the largest community between Seattle and Minneapolis. Situated amid farmland, the town feels more like a mid-western city than an urban center in the Pacific Northwest.

One of the highlights of Spokane is Riverfront Park. Bike paths and picnic areas that frame the dramatic Spokane Falls flank the Spokane River. Most of the summit and flanks of nearby 5,881-foot Mount Spokane, an outliner of the Selkirk Mountains, are within 16,000-acre Mount Spokane State Park, a favorite area for hiking in summer and skiing in winter. Just south of Spokane lies the 17,000-acre Turnbull National Wildlife Refuge. Unlike other refuges, this one isn't open to hunting, and thus provides a safe area for hiking and wildlife observation during the autumn.

South of Spokane, one enters the Palouse Prairie region of Washington. Glacial dust known as loess was piled thick over the region, creating drought soils that resisted colonization by trees. Even though the region receives more than 25 inches of precipitation – which is more than ample for tree growth – it remains a largely treeless expanse. Instead, prior to settlement dense grasslands covered the area. Today, most of the Palouse has been plowed up and planted to a domestic grass we call wheat. Indeed, it is one of the major wheat growing regions in the country. Small farming communities dot this beautiful rolling land.

One of the best places to get a bird's eye view of this special farming region is from Steptoe Butte, an isolated outcrop of the Selkirk Mountains that has resisted erosion. The top of the mountain is within Steptoe Butte State Park and provides a panoramic view of the patterned fields below.

Pullman is the largest city in the Palouse region. Despite its nickname as the "lentil capital of the world," Pullman is more than an agricultural processing center. With more than 16,000 students, Pullman's Washington State University is a major influence on the community's character and offers more than 100 fields of study.

Tucannon River Valley in southeastern Washington

Opposite: Wheat fields near Colfax

Along the Snake River in southeast Washington is Clarkston. It lies just across the river from Lewiston, Idaho. The towns are named for the leaders of the Lewis and Clark Expedition that traveled through the region in 1805 and 1806. The two towns owe some of their economic prosperity to barge traffic on the Snake and Columbia Rivers. Ocean going vessels come upstream to this point to pick up shipments of wheat, lumber and other products from the "Inland Empire."

West of Clarkston is Walla Walla. The town with its tree-lined streets, old homes, and beautiful parks is like an oasis in the midst of wheat fields. Some of the trees are among the largest in Washington, including one 21-foot diameter catalpa tree on the Whitman College campus. The Whitman Mission National Historic Site, seven miles west of Walla Walla commemorates the first white settlement in the region. Dr. Marcus Whitman established a mission here in 1836. Whitman, along with his wife, was killed by the Indians 11 years later. Despite its location in the middle of agricultural fields, its biggest industry may well be education – Walla Walla boasts three colleges – Whitman College, Walla Walla College and Walla Walla Community College.

Just south of Walla Walla are the Blue Mountains. Mostly in Oregon, a small segment of the range extends into Washington. With thick forests and deep grassy canyons, the Blue Mountains are an island of wildness in the midst of agricultural lands.

Washington state is no longer a backwater of the country, but is now considered one of its most vibrant and exciting areas. With a booming economy, growing Asian trade, and physically one of the most attractive states in the nation, Washington is what most of the rest of the country would like to be. Yet for all its optimism and growth, Washington still retains elements of its more rural past, and friendly ways. In most respects, it has the best of both worlds.

About the Author/Photographer

George Wuerthner is the author of 23 books, including *Beautiful America's Alaska*. A freelance writer, photographer and ecologist, Wuerthner wears multiple hats. His articles and photography have appeared in numerous regional and national publications including *National Geographic*, *Natural History*, *Outside*, *Outdoor Photography*, *Adirondack Life*, *Arizona Highways*, *Sierra*, *New York Times* and many others. His photography has been displayed at the Smithsonian and a traveling show on the environment that was seen throughout Europe.

In addition to writing and photography, Wuerthner guides natural history tours, teaches photography workshops and field ecology courses. He also works as a geographic consultant to National Geographic and as a biological consultant to the Nature Conservancy, among others.

In the past, he has worked as a high school teacher, rare plant botanist, wildlife biologist, river ranger and park ranger.

Today he resides in Eugene, Oregon with his wife, Mollie, and two children, all of whom are enthusiastic outdoors persons and often accompany George on his frequent photography expeditions. Son Stratton, now three, went on his first backpack trip when he was three-weeks-old. Five-year-old daughter Summer was hiking up to four miles a day when she was only two, and has already hiked extensively in the Olympic National Park and the Mount Rainier National Park.

Mount Deception, Olympic National Park

Back Cover: Rhododendrons at University of Washington